Introduction

Making button jewelry is fast and easy fun that can be enjoyed by crafters of all ages. Button jewelry can be made inexpensively using "found" items as a base or those purchased at craft and fabric stores.

Most homes have a button box or button tin. This is where all the lost buttons are stored, waiting in vain to be stitched back onto their original garment. The number of buttons in the box continues to grow because replacing lost buttons is not as exciting as stitching or crafting a new project. Also added to the button box are extra buttons left over from those purchased on cards or those cut from worn-out garments by a frugal seamstress.

Old buttons add a delightful accent to this fashionable jewelry. You may be lucky enough to inherit a "button box" or two. You can also add to this treasure by purchasing bags of old buttons at flea markets or thrift stores. Combining old buttons with inexpensive strips of new buttons, you can make a wide variety of pins, bracelets, and accessories.

Home sewers, quilters, and all types of stitchers will enjoy making jewelry that when worn identifies their hobby and interest. Joggers, hikers, and other enthusiasts who participate in a physical activity or sport have special clothes and accessories. Now quilters and stitchers can wear a special piece of jewelry that reveals their "hot button."

Laura Elizabeth

History

The word "button" comes from the French word *bouton,* which means "something pushed out." Buttons have been sewn on clothes as fasteners and ornaments for many centuries. Bone buttons found in museums are older than written history. Buttons and studs of brass have been found in graves of Egyptians who lived 2,500 years before the birth of Christ.

Buttons in many cultures sometimes represent traditions. The Chinese used to wear five buttons on their coats, each one representing the five virtues taught by Confucius: humility, justice, order, prudence, and rectitude.

Buttons became popular about 1200–1300 when fitted clothes came into fashion. Previous to that, robes and loose gowns were tied by strings or girdles or fastened with jeweled pins. Many buttons that are now ornamental once served a useful purpose, such as the sleeve buttons on men's coats. These represent the buttons that were originally used to fasten the lace frills at the bottom of shirt sleeves to the coat. The buttons on the back of men's long-tailed cutaway coats were designed to hold up the coattails when men rode on horseback.

The buttons on men's clothes used to be sewn on the left side as they are on women's clothes. Men's buttons were moved to the right side during the Middle Ages so that a man could unbutton his coat quickly with his left hand and draw his sword with his right hand.

There are two basic types of buttons: one type having holes for stitching thread through and another type featuring a shank of metal or cloth through which the thread is sewn to attach the button.

Buttons are used on many clothes today, although the zipper has replaced many of the buttons that were once used. Today, buttons are made from a variety of materials, including mother-of-pearl, vegetable ivory, bone, metal, wood, paper, leather, plastic, shell, stone, and glass. More expensive ornamental buttons are made of pewter, silver, or gold.

Most buttons today are made of vegetable ivory. Vegetable ivory is the name given to the nut which grows on the ivory-nut palm tree. The nuts are harvested and shelled by machinery that also removes the kernels. When heated, the nut becomes as hard as stone and looks like ivory. It can be dyed to match any cloth color.

Old buttons exhibit detail and craftsmanship not found today. One or two used as an embellishment on jewelry make wonderful fashion accessories.

Supplies and Materials

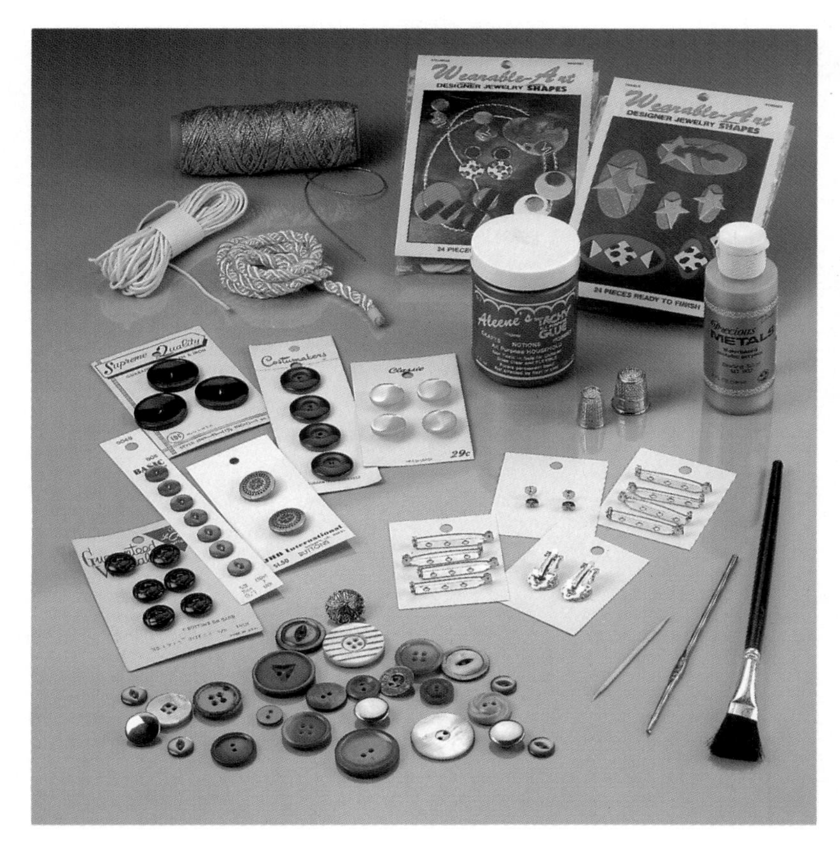

Pin Bases: A variety of objects can be used as the base to which buttons are glued. The size of the base you choose will determine the finished size of the pin. Mini-slates, wood shapes, old or new buckles, juice-can lids, ceramic bases, silver concha shapes, old jewelry or a metal pin (campaign or slogan type) that already has a back on it. There are endless possibilities, limited only by your own imagination. Die-cut shapes from jewelry board are available in packages of various shapes from the Wearable Art Company and can be found in craft stores. Rounds, ovals, hearts, squares, and rectangles from this line have been used for several of the pins photographed. Coordinating earrings can be made from the smaller-sized shapes. For each shape of pin, study the photograph of possible bases and then use the one most accessible to you.

Pin Backs: These are glued to the back of the base so that the pin may be secured to a garment. Select a good-quality pin back with a sharp tip so it will not snag clothing. Available in a variety of sizes at craft stores.

Earring Posts and Backs or Earring Clips: Glue these to the back of buttons to create earrings that will match your jewelry. Available at craft and hobby stores.

Ring Bases: Use to make a special button into a ring. Available at hobby stores along with other jewelry findings.

Buttons—Old and New: Cards of matching buttons can be purchased at fabric stores. Use these to cover your base, adding old buttons or a special new button as an accent.

Jewelry: Old jewelry can be used as a base on which to glue your buttons. You may want to disassemble costume jewelry or broken watches and use the parts in your button collage (see page 14).

Sewing Notions: A variety of sewing notions can be used to fill in small spaces or add an interesting accent to your button collage. Use snaps, hooks and eyes, rivets, grommets, zipper pulls, beads, and charms.

Metallic Paint: This paint is used to cover the pin base when using metallic buttons. Available at craft stores.

Craft Paint: Use this paint for covering the pin base when using colored buttons. Available at craft stores.

Aleene's Tacky Glue: This is a permanent bonding glue, available in a wide-mouth plastic jar, which will secure all types of buttons to a base. Apply with a toothpick. Available at craft stores.

Elastic Thread and Elastic Gimp: A mesh crocheted from this thread is used for button bracelets. Gold elastic gimp is available from craft stores.

Button Cord or Dental Floss: Use an extra-strong button cord or dental floss to string buttons for necklaces.

Sorting and Storing Buttons

All buttons, old and new, look wonderful in old glass canning jars set on a sunny windowsill. Remove new buttons from cards, discarding clamps or thread that hold them to the cards, and add to jars.

It is easier to construct a button project if buttons are sorted by color or type. Use a large jar for white buttons, then smaller jars for various colored, clear, or metal buttons.

Basic Button Collage Pin

1. Select button color or category for the pin you will be making. Sort buttons by size. Set aside any special buttons or accents to use as a focal point.
2. Select base. Paint base to match buttons, if necessary.
3. Glue small, flat buttons over surface of base to create a foundation for collage. Use inexpensive strips of new buttons for this bottom layer. Most of these buttons will be covered by a top layer of buttons, so it is unnecessary to use a great variety of buttons.
4. Add another layer of buttons, overlapping interesting sizes and shapes. Using special buttons or accents, create a focal point. Shank butttons work best when glued to the top layer of buttons, so that the shank can be arranged between the empty spaces in the lower layer of buttons. Add any interesting embellishments you desire: snaps, hooks, zipper pulls, beads, charms, or other sewing notions.
5. Glue pin back to back of base.

Step 1

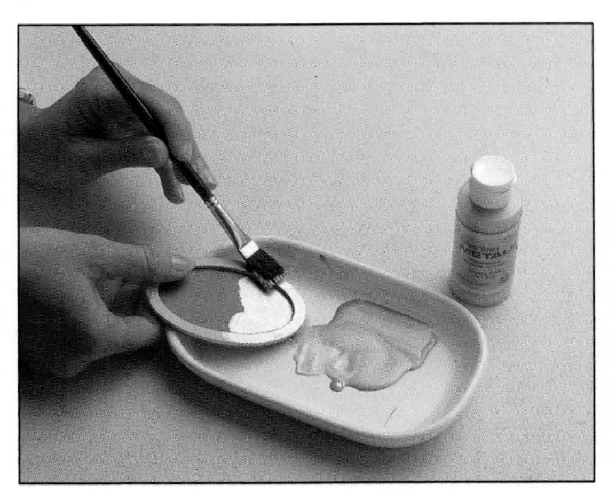

Step 2

Step 3

Step 4

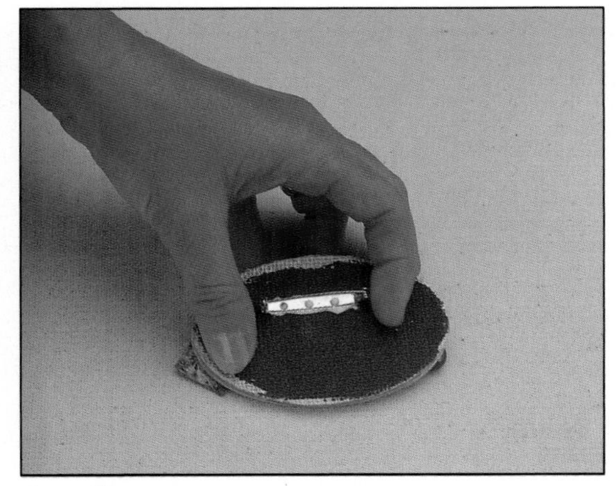

Step 5

Hot Button Pin Ideas

Round Pins

Base possibilities: juice-can lid, mini-slate, designer jewelry shape, large button, colored ceramic base, or metal pin with backing.

Round button pins have a focal point placed off-center. Porcelain flowers add interest to the light blue pin.

Oval Pins

Base possibilities: mini-slate, designer jewelry shape, pin base for jewelry, metallic base for concha jewelry.

A special carved deer button, along with carved bone buttons, accents this brown pin. Metal buttons are glued to the metallic base used to make concha jewelry, while brass buttons decorate a pin backing. Matching earrings are made by attaching an earring back to special buttons.

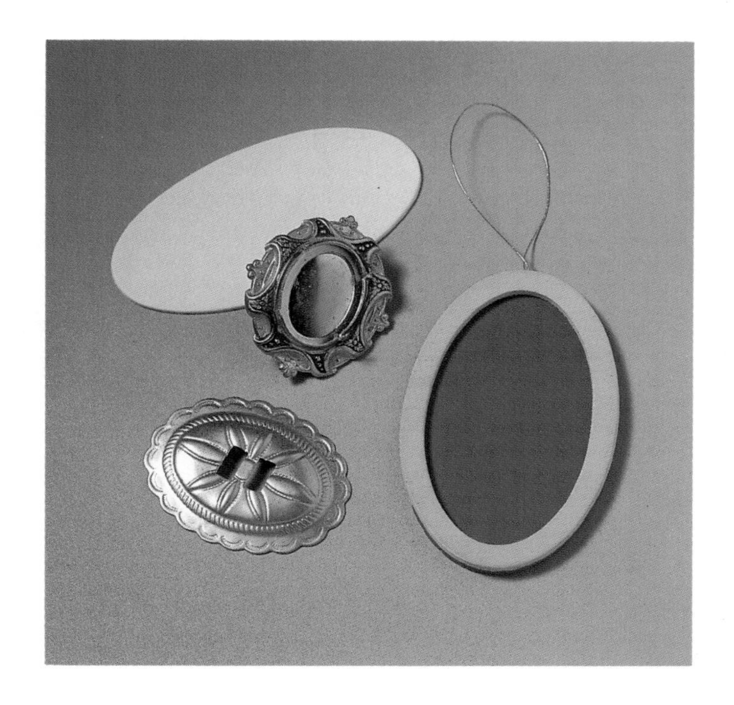

Heart-Shaped Pins

Base possibilities: wood shapes and designer jewelry shapes of various sizes.

Various sizes and shapes of hearts make delightful pins. Matching earrings can be made by gluing tiny buttons to small-sized hearts.

Rectangular- and Square-Shaped Pins

Base possibilities: designer jewelry shapes of various sizes.

Spectacular pins with matching earrings use a variety of buttons.

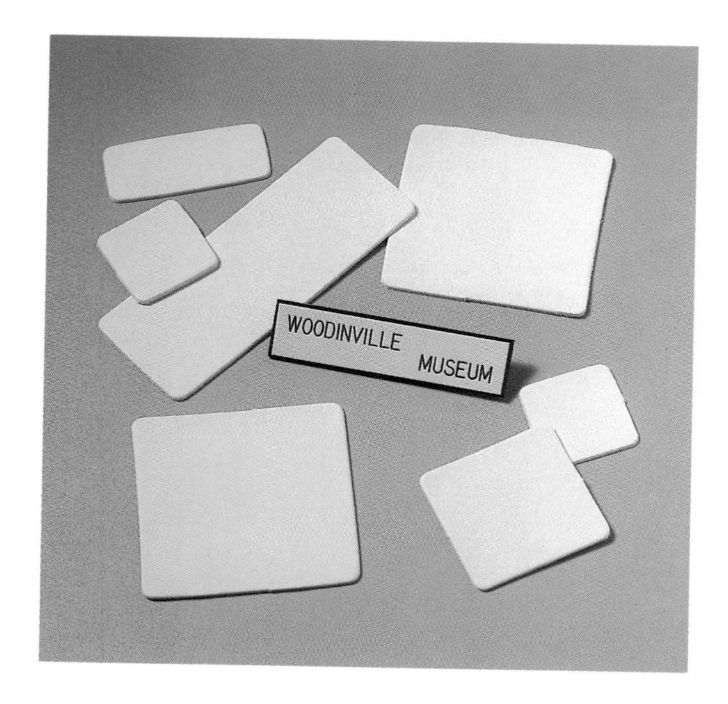

Buckle Base Pins

Base possibilities: New plastic buckles, antique buckles. Press sculpting clay or glue designer jewelry shape behind open space to fill in base.

Antique buckles serve as a frame for special metal buttons. A colorful plastic polka-dot buckle features brightly colored buttons.

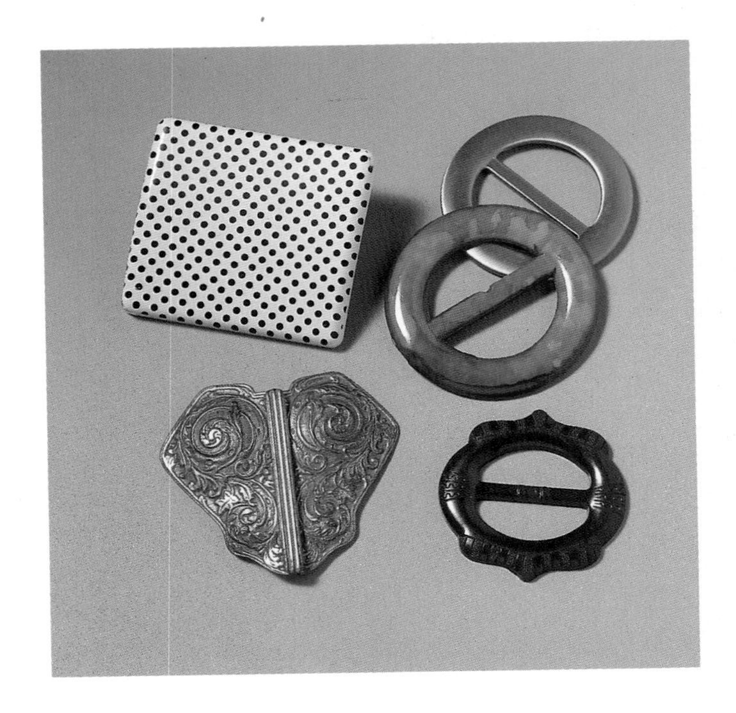

Stitcher's Special Pins

Base possibilities: oval mini-slate, large button, or designer jewelry shape.

Thimbles, needles, hooks, snaps, various metallic sewing notions, and quilt block pins create a special accessory for stitchers.

Costume Jewelry Pins

Base possibilities: oval mini-slate, old jewelry, antique buckles.

Parts of old watches or jewelry can enhance button pins.

Necklaces

Special Button Pin and Necklace

Sometimes a single button is so special that it can stand on its own with little embellishment. Simply attach a small pin back to a shank button and wear it as a pin or decorative accent. Or thread a 7″ length of ¼″-wide pastel picot-edge ribbon through the buttonhole of a mother-of-pearl button with interesting colorations and tie into a small bow. Attach a small pin back for wearing. Use the same idea and attach to small barrettes to make decorative accents for hair.

A single button can also be worn on a pretty ribbon as a necklace. Using 1 yard of ¼″-wide or ⅛″-wide picot-edge ribbon, thread each end through the buttonholes of a special mother-of-pearl button. Tie into a small bow and wear as a pendant with button and bow in front. You can change the ribbon to match your wardrobe.

Treasure Necklace

Materials
1 yd. woven cording
2 8-mm bell caps
1 barrel clasp
1 package eye pins
2 yds. 1/16″-wide narrow ribbon
4 tiny spools of thread
Various treasures: thimbles, "worry" dolls, old rings, bobbins, bells, charms, and beads
Aleene's Tacky Glue

DIRECTIONS
1. Cut woven cording to 30″ or desirable length. Dab each end with glue and attach bell caps. Attach one part of barrel clasp to each bell cap.
2. Divide treasures into groups. Large treasures are attached directly to cord with eye pins. Divide smaller treasures, including spools of thread, into pairs and tie securely to each end of a 4″ piece of ribbon. Dab each knot with glue to secure.
3. Begin in center of cord and work toward sides, attaching each large treasure to necklace with eye pin. Push eye pin through cording. Bend to secure on back side of cording, catching the middle of a 4″ piece of ribbon that has a smaller treasure or bead secured to each end.
4. Slide inexpensive rings over cording between treasures.

Basic Button Necklace

Materials
Needle with large eye
Strong button cord or dental floss
100 buttons (approx.)
Assorted beads from broken jewelry
Barrel clasp or hook closing
Glue

DIRECTIONS
1. Thread a large-eye needle with button cord or dental floss.
2. String 100 buttons on cord. Use just 1 hole on 2- or 4-hole buttons. To spotlight special buttons or utilize shank buttons, attach 2 shank buttons back to back. First, thread button cord through each eye, forming a small loop; then run cord through this loop.

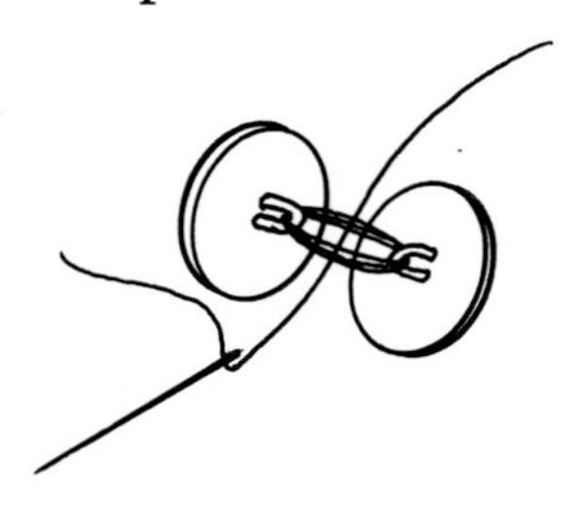

3. Use old beads or small buttons at ends of necklace so that it will lie flat on back of neck when worn.
4. Knot securely, attaching each end to clasp, and add a dab of glue to secure knot.

Bracelets

Elastic Bracelet

Materials
1 roll gold elastic gimp
Crochet hook, size 7
Needle with large eye
51 (approx.) metal or colored shank-type buttons

DIRECTIONS
1. Crochet a mesh base on which to secure buttons, following directions and illustrations:
   a. Using elastic gimp, chain 55 stitches. Add more or fewer stitches, depending on your tension, to make chain the size of your wrist.
   b. Add 3 rows of double crochet for the mesh. Knot and weave in tail of elastic.
2. Thread a large-eye needle with elastic gimp. Beginning along one edge, weave elastic gimp through mesh, adding a button each time needle is on top of mesh. Without knotting elastic, continue weaving through second and third row. Knot securely.

CREATIVE OPTION: For those who wish to wear their elastic button bracelet over their watch (it makes a wonderful accent piece for a sport watch), leave an opening in the middle row of crochet stitches, as illustrated.

Narrow Elastic Bracelet

Materials
Elastic cord
Needle with large eye
35 (approx.) metal or colored shank-type buttons

DIRECTIONS
1. Thread a large-eye needle with elastic cord.
2. String approximately 35 shank-type buttons on cord.
3. Cut ends a comfortable length and knot securely.

CROCHET DIRECTIONS

Chain Stitch: Make a slip knot on hook. Wrap hook around long length of yarn and pull it through the loop.

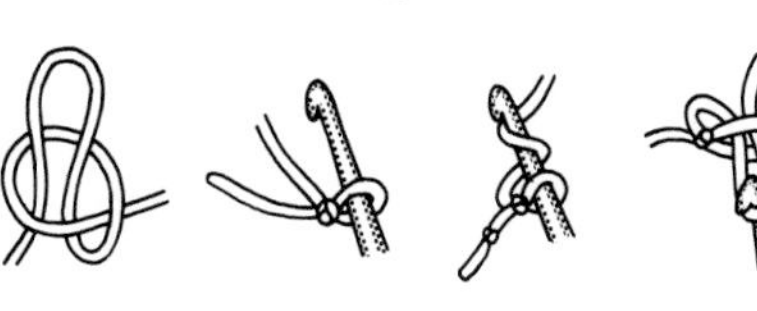

Double Crochet: With one loop on hook, loop yarn around hook and insert hook into a stitch. Hook long length of yarn and pull it through the stitch (you now have 3 loops on hook). Hook yarn again and pull it through 2 loops; hook again and pull through remaining 2 loops.

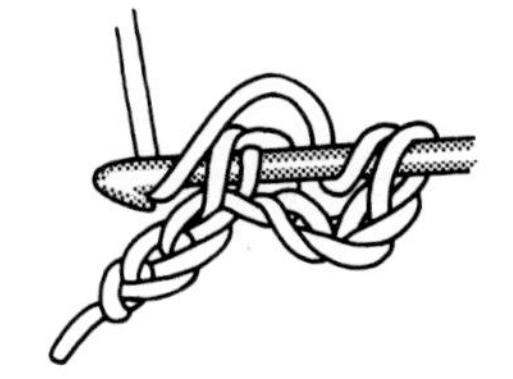

Metal Clamp Bracelet

Materials
Metal clamp-type or bangle bracelet
30 (approx.) metallic buttons
Aleene's Tacky Glue

DIRECTIONS

Securely glue metal buttons to stable part of bracelet, the part that will not bend when bracelet is put over wrist.

Fashionable Accessories

Stick Pin, Tie Bar, Scarf Pin, Ring, Pendant, Barrette

Purchase an inexpensive piece of jewelry or a barrette and glue on buttons for decoration.

Treasure Chests

Button Safe

Materials
Half-pint quilted jelly jar and lid
Core from paper towel roll
Assorted buttons
Small felt scrap
Aleene's Tacky Glue

DIRECTIONS
1. Cut paper towel core to fit inside jelly jar. Cover with felt.
2. Glue buttons to felt-covered core.
3. Glue large button to inside bottom of jelly jar. Dab glue on one end of button-covered core and insert in jelly jar. You have now created a "safe" inside your buttons to store your family jewels or "mad money."
4. Glue metal buttons to lid in area not covered by jar ring.
5. Screw jar ring on top of jar lid.

Dressing Table Jar

Materials
Decorative glass jar with lid
1 large glass button
Assorted buttons, including metallic and small, white pearlized buttons
Small doily
Aleene's Tacky Glue

DIRECTIONS
1. Glue large glass button to center of jar lid.
2. Add several rows of metallic buttons.
3. Add small, white pearlized buttons, overlapping previous rows.
4. Glue a pretty metal button to top of clear glass button in center of jar.
5. To hide underside of buttons and glue, dab a small amount of glue on one side of small doily and position on inside of jar lid.

Storing Button Jewelry

"Pin" Cushion

Materials
¼ yd. ecru fabric
Doily, 5½" diameter, or piece of crochet work 7" x 7" or larger
¾ yd. ½"-wide ecru ruffled lace trim
Polyester stuffing
¼ yd. ¼"-wide ecru ribbon
Special pin (optional)

DIRECTIONS
1. Cut two 6½" x 6½" squares from ecru fabric for back and front of pin cushion.
2. Center doily on pin cushion front. Tack in place by hand to secure. If using crochet work, machine stitch to pin cushion front ¼" from all raw edges of fabric. Cut away any excess crochet work.

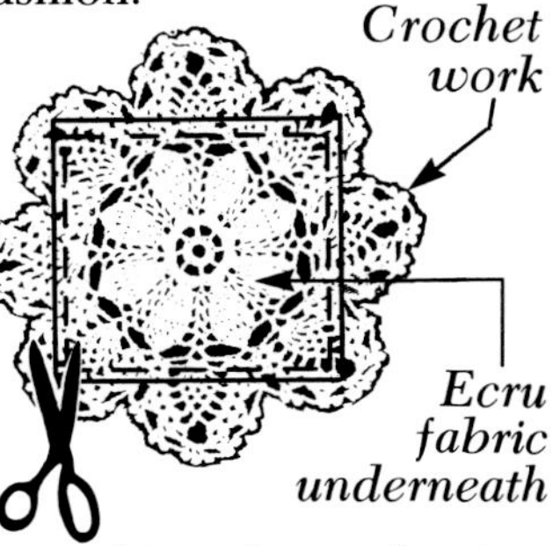

3. Baste lace trim to pin cushion front, having finished edge toward inside and raw edges even.
4. Stitch pin cushion front to pin cushion back in a ¼" seam around outside edges, leaving an opening for turning.
5. Turn pin cushion to right side. Stuff with polyester stuffing. Slip-stitch opening closed.
6. Tie ribbon into a small bow and tack to corner of pin cushion.
7. Pin a special pin to the top and give as a gift or use as a special storage place for an heirloom pin that you have made.

"Pin" Sash

The pin sash lets you attractively display all of your button treasures when you are not wearing them.

Materials
Wooden cafe curtain ring, 3" diameter
1 yd. 2"-wide moire-type ribbon
Aleene's Tacky Glue

DIRECTIONS
1. Thread ribbon through wooden cafe ring, folding near center. Glue ribbon "tails" to each other near wooden ring.
2. Attach your special pins to tails and hang on wall.

Home Decor

Picture Frames

Base possibilities: wooden, metal, plastic or fabric picture frame.

For a man's photograph, use wooden, leather, or military buttons to add a masculine touch on a wood picture frame. Mother-of-pearl buttons, including some from baby clothes, decorate an ivorine oval frame holding a child's photo. Metallic buttons are used to highlight the corners of a metallic picture frame.

That Patchwork Place, Inc.
is proud to introduce its new line of creative craft books

❖ Laura Elizabeth™ ❖

These books contain creative, fun-type projects that can be quickly and easily made for year-round gifts or home decor. Both timely and fashion conscious, these projects have the same easy-to-follow instructions and illustrations that you have come to expect from That Patchwork Place. You can be assured the completed projects will look like those shown in the gorgeous photos.

Folded Fabric Fun
Make a wide variety of projects using a simple method that substitutes folded fabric for sewing. You can easily duplicate many of your favorite quilt patterns in three different sizes to create a multitude of projects. Construct the small size for Christmas ornaments or mug rugs; use larger sizes to make potholders, hot pads, towel tops, pillows, totes, or purses. Pick the method of assembly that you prefer: hand sewing, machine sewing, glue stick or Wonder-Under™. Easy-to-follow directions for several finishing techniques also offer individual choices for crafters of all levels. L600, 32 pp.

It Makes Scents
Scented projects are perfect for Christmas decorations or gifts. You'll love the scented Spicy Santa, Spicy Sally and the Spicy Christmas Angel. All have cinnamon-stick arms and legs and bodies stuffed with scented herbs. Good smells will come from your kitchen when you make herb vinegar, herbal soup bags, mug rugs, crafty cookies, a gingerbread-man garland, spicy casserole cozies (in three common sizes) and even a hot pad that releases its fragrance when a warm dish is placed on it. Have fun making your own floral swags, garlands and wreaths as well as ornaments with the popular country look, using paper ribbon, dried materials and lace. Other projects to delight your senses include scented padded hangers, sachets, potpourri, dried apple wreaths and ornaments, and scented lace pillows. L601, 32 pp.

ISBN 0-943574-71-4
9 780943 574714

SCHOLASTIC

GRADES 3 & UP

Answer the question

Elaborate thinking

ACE

Cite evidence

Short-Response WRITING

15 Mini-Lessons, Strategies, and Scaffolds to Help Students Craft Meaningful Short Responses

Includes Test-Taking Strategies

GRACE LONG